Poetry:
Life, Love, and Death

By
Nichole Williams

Table of Contents

Dedication

I would like to dedicate this book to my husband for all his support and motivation in getting published.

About the Author

Nichole is married with six children, 3 dogs, and a cat. She spends her days with her husband and children when she is not working her full-time job as a property manager. Nichole loves being outdoors most days, but when inside, she loves to be curled up with a good book or watching crime TV.

What is Love?

Love is a smile on your face.

Love is the feeling of butterflies in your stomach.

It is not tears.

It is not hurt,

Nor secrets from each other.

Love is a bond, unable to be broken.

Flowers

A symbol of love.

A symbol of heartfelt kindness.

Sincere apologies.

Sympathetic well wishes.

A flower in a garden.

A flower to brighten your home.

A flower to recognize every month, every birthday.

A garden of flowers for the honeybees and butterflies.

What is a flower?

Footprints

It all began with one tiny ultrasound.

She showed me your tiny little feet and your
tiny little toes.

When you were born, your footprint was
stamped into a piece of paper. A constant
reminder of how tiny you were.

Before I knew it, you were walking. Then running.

Riding a bike. Driving a car.

But that tiny little footprint will forever
be imprinted on my heart.

The Way You Look Tonight

I look at you like a child sees a rainbow, a puppy, their
eyes lighting up on Christmas morning.

The way I look at you, is as if you owned the world.
You are my world.

Looking into your eyes. They glisten like the diamond on
my finger.

The way you look tonight, is the way I always see you.
Flawless.

Love

Open your eyes.

Open your heart.

Love yourself first.

Believe in yourself first.

Love will be seen, felt, heard.

When it is real love, you do not have to try.

It will not be forced.

Do not be afraid.

Let him love you. You deserve the very best.

Losing

Is it real?

Am I dreaming?

Wake me up when February ends.

This can't be real.

No one can prepare you.

Losing a loved one.

The one you grew up looking up to.

The one who taught you about life, girls,
baseball, how to love.

When you lose your dad or any parent, you
lose a part of you forever.

No one teaches you how to cope or how to
handle death.

You learn on your own.

To talk about them often.

Take pictures while they are still around.

Listen to their words, their voice.

Cherish every moment.

Kids

Tiny humans to provide for.

To love, clothe, feed.

They get bigger and say, "I can do it all by myself."

So you let them.

Let them grow.

Let them learn.

Learn from experiences.

Learn from lessons and mistakes made.

There is no owner's manual or how-to.

Every day is a new day and you hope you did your best.

Then the day comes.

They graduate.

You release them into the real world.

Spread your wings, little one.

I know you will do big things.

Live your life.

Live your dream.

Love At First Sight

Is it real love?

Is it true love?

Is it lust?

Does love at first sight exist?

I didn't think it did until I met you.

You showed me true love.

You showed me how to be myself, how to open up.

The moment I saw you, I knew it was love at first sight.

That first look into your eyes.

I knew it was you.

Forever and always.

Summer Time

Fresh fruit.

Summer sun.

The smell of green grass.

Popsicles by the pool.

Flashlight tag with friends.

Bonfires and s'mores.

Floating down the river.

Sweet tea on the front porch.

Summer Time.

Baseball

Summertime.

Late nights.

Nine innings.

Three strikes out.

Hot dogs, Nachos. Peanuts.

Summer nights.

Cheering on your favorite team.

Baseball.

Home.

The Wedding

We met so many years ago.

That night, I will never forget.

It led to the rest of forever.

We dated, but not for long.

We both knew this was it.

You took me to our favorite place.

You got down on one knee and asked me to marry you.

I cried as I said, "YES!"

I knew you were it, forever, for always.

We planned and planned.

Invitations went out.

All our favorite people cheered us on.

The day had finally come.

You stood there and stared as I walked down the aisle.

The look in your eyes I will never forget.

I love you, my husband.

Today. Tomorrow. Forever.

Her

The number in your phone.

The lipstick on your shirt.

The smell of perfume as you walk in the door
late every night.

It wasn't my number.

It wasn't my lipstick.

Why wasn't I enough?

Did I hurt you?

Could I have been a better girlfriend?

Don't say you're sorry.

It's too late for that.

I'm not falling for the same mistake twice.

She can have you now.

I deserve better.

You and Me

It's you and me
against the world.

Nothing stopping us.

Nothing standing in our way.

Our love is so strong.

Indestructible. Unbreakable.

It's you and me.

Forever, for always.

One team.

One love.

Lost Girl

What did I do?

Why did you leave?

You tell me you love me; then you walk away.

I'm lost in this world without you.

I thought I was your whole world.

Ten years passed, and you just walked away,
disappeared.

No one to talk to.

No one to turn to.

No one to lean on.

I'm scared.

I'm alone.

I'm a lost girl.

Summer Time

It's 3:01. The last bell rings.

School is out for summer.

It's the weekend.

It's seven days a week.

The next three months.

Swimming, baseball, a trip to the
beach.

The days of summer, we don't want to
end.

Suntans and lemonade stands.

Summer time.

Family

What makes a family?

Is it birth?

Is it blood relatives?

Is it a best friend?

Family can be blood but shut them out if
they do you wrong.

Family is a best friend, who is there for you.

A mom and dad creating a new life.

Family is four legs and kisses that welcome
you home every day.

Family is love. Family is home.

I Once Was Loved

I once was loved,
Then was left,
Once again loved,
and once again left.

I once was loved.
This time for good.
I was finally loved.
As no one else ever had.

I once was loved,
By the man I thought would last.
I once was loved,
We said it would last like nothing else ever could.

I once was loved,
by the kindest man.
I once was loved,
by the gentlest man.

I once was loved,
by the man I married.
I once was loved,
And his child I carried.

I once was loved,
but not anymore.
I once was loved,
I can cry no more.

I once was loved,
by the man of my dreams.
I once was loved,
For so long it seemed.

I once was loved,
Oh, how I cried.
I once was loved,
by my man who died.

I am still loved,
by his baby so dear.
I am still loved,
By his family who is near.

I once was loved,
forever I thought.
I am still loved,
by his heart I took.

I once was loved,
forever and ever.
I am still loved,
Forever and Always.

I am still loved,
In one special way.
I am still loved,
I know one day I will be ok.

Words

Love. Anger.

Respect. Hate.

Trust. Guilt.

What do these words express?

A person's feelings and emotions.

Anxiety. Depression.

Hope. Fear.

Compassion. Contentment.

All feelings everyone experiences.

In relationships, friendships, everyday life.

From work to family.

A person can experience these different feelings.

These words describe a human being, their actions, personalities.

These words can make a person think and act the way they do.

Words.

Blue

Blue can be so many different things.

Blue is a color.

Blue is the sky.

Blue is depression.

Blue is a car.

Blue is a storm.

Blue is a rainbow.

Blue is a flower.

Blue is a favorite mug.

Blue is a favorite shirt.

Blue is the name of a family pet.

Blue is anything you want it to be.

A sunrise.

A sunset.

Life, death.

More than just a color.

Blue.

The Last Fight

Those words you said,

they hurt so bad.

Those fists you threw,

the marks remain.

Did I say something wrong?

What started the fight?

I will never know what made you so angry.

You've said hurtful words before.

You've thrown fists before.

But this time was different.

This was the last fight.

I survived long enough to tell my story.

I survived long enough to see you punished.

You'll never hurt another.

This was your last fight.

I survived your words.

I survived your hands.

I am making sure you never hurt another.

This was your last fight.

I survived.

You lost.

The Weekend

What is a weekend?

Let's party.

Let's celebrate.

Let's barbeque.

Let's swim.

Some float.

Some work.

Some hike.

Some bike.

Weekends are for being lazy.

Weekends are for reading and relaxing.

Weekends are for the kids.

Weekends are for trips taken.

We can bike and skate.

We can walk and hike.

We can see a movie, go to dinner.

We can get together with friends, play a few games.

When is your weekend?

Where will you go?

Life

What does your life look like?

Let's explore.

Some work, some travel.

Some stay home all day.

Some spend their day with family.

Life is about living every day to its fullest.

Work. Kids. Travel. Explore.

Hang out with friends.

Make plans.

Buy a pet.

Is life about living?

Is life a game?

Where is your playing piece?

What stage of life are you on?

The Last Day

Today, I was told, is my last day to live.

Twenty-four hours left.

My heart aches for those I am leaving behind.

Did I live my life to its fullest?

Did I travel enough, complete my life plans,

say "I love you" enough?

Did I forgive enough, laugh enough, cry enough?

What will I do with only one day left to

live?

I will live it to its fullest.

Eat all the food, play all the games, make

one last visit to my parents, friends, family.

I can't tell them why.

I can't cry. Can't be sad.

I have to hold my head up and be strong for them.

Tomorrow will come, and I will be gone.

Will my family be sad?

Will they mourn?

Will they miss me?

Will my friends come to say goodbye and pay respects?

Will I be forgotten?

Will I live on in memories, stories, and pictures?

So many questions with only twenty-four

hours to live

I can't say anything.

No "goodbyes", only "I love you".

Are you ready to say goodbye?

Did you live out your life?

What would you do with one last day to live?

Today More Than Yesterday

"Do you love me?" I ask all too often.

"Yes, of course?" is always the response I get.

But why do I keep asking this?

Because I have a past.

I have been traumatized.

I fear being left again.

"Do you love me?" I ask again.

His response?

"I love you today more than yesterday, and I will love you more tomorrow. I will remind you and show you how much I love you until the day I die."

The Last Kiss

It's time to say goodbye.

It's time to say good night.

Every kiss is an apology for the hurt you have inflicted

earlier in the day.

I cannot take any more hurt.

I cannot take any more fear.

I cannot take any more apologies.

I am done.

I am walking out the door.

When you wake, you will not find me.

I won't be here anymore.

I am done.

Tonight was the last good night.

The last goodbye.

The last kiss

The Porch

Here I sit, relaxing on my porch.

I take it all in.

The rain, the air, my dogs, my kids, my husband, my life.

I sip my coffee slowly, watching the rain come down.

I could not imagine a life different from my life now.

I am happy, at peace, and in love.

I sit here on my porch, thankful for it all.

This feeling inside me, it's new.

I finally know that I am home.

Back To School

Today, she left for kindergarten.

Her shoes, tied tight.

Her backpack on.

So excited, ready to make new friends.

Today, she heads to middle school.

She still lets me snap a picture.

We pick up her friends on the way.

Today, she heads to high school.

Her backpack on, she is ready to go.

"Don't forget to take a pic", she says.

Today, she catches a ride with friends.

Today, she leaves for her senior year.

Where have the last twelve years gone?

I cry.

She says it will be ok, it's just school.

She drives herself, grabbing coffee on the way.

But first, I get my last, first day of school picture.

Back to school.

Thirteen years.

Kindergarten to senior year.

Hug them tight.

Take that picture.

It all goes by so fast.

Life

Your parents met by chance.

They love each other dearly.

Nine months later, you come along.

An unconditional love from both your parents, mother and father.

You grow, learn, and develop.

You go to school.

Make lifelong friends.

Graduate.

Go to college.

Get a job.

Go out for coffee.

You meet someone.

A man who will one day become your husband.

This meeting happened by chance.

You both fall in love.

Get married.

Nine months later, you are holding your very own baby girl.

All by chance.

All with love.

The circle of life.

Thoughts

You got the news today.

Your brain doesn't stop racing.

So many thoughts.

So many things you still want to do.

So many places you still want to see.

If only you had more time.

"Why did this have to happen to me?" you think.

You have a family, a husband, children too.

"Will they be ok without me?"

The thoughts run wild in your head.

What do you say?

How do you feel?

You haven't been sick.

"Why me? Why now?"

You say it over and over in your head until

you're ready to share the news with your family.

"I have cancer. I have cancer. I have cancer."

What thoughts are going through your mind now?

Will you accept it?

Will you find peace?

Will you fight?

Will you survive?

These are your thoughts now.

I Love You, My Child

I carried you for nine months.

You heard my heartbeat for nine months.

Now, I carry you close.

You still hear my heartbeat and you instantly calm.

You are my mini, and I am your momma.

I will hold you close, protect you, wipe away your tears.

I am forever your mother.

You are forever my child.

I love you today, tomorrow, Always.

I love you, my child.

Home

I have a car.

I have a job.

I have a house.

Something is still missing.

I adopt a cat.

I adopt a dog.

Something is still missing.

I go for coffee.

I go for walks.

Something is still missing.

I meet someone.

We go for coffee.

We go for walks.

Something is no longer missing.

I fell in love.

That void is filled.

He loves what I love.

Something is no longer missing.

We go on trips.

We go for coffee.

I meet his friends, he meets mine.

Something is no longer missing.

He has brought me peace.

He has brought me happiness.

He has brought me contentment.

I am finally home.

I found my home in him.

A home is not a house.

A home is not an object thing.

Home is where you feel happy, calm, and content.

Home is where your heart is.

I am home.

You are my home.

Ashes

I received the call today.

Your ashes were ready to be picked up.

A pool of emotions ran through me as I hung up the

phone.

I still can't believe you're gone.

It's been two weeks since the accident.

You were my whole world.

Now you are ashes on my mantle.

I wear your wedding band around my neck.

Next to your wedding band is a ring filled with your

ashes.

Now, I feel a little closer to you.

Life will never be the same.

You were the love of my life.

Now you are ashes.

The Rules of Life

Be kind always.

Just being kind may make someone else's day.

Being kind leaves no room for bullying and negativity.

Avoid negativity.

Forget the negative thoughts.

Forget the negative people.

Leave the negative situations.

Never give up.

Giving up is failing.

Giving up is losing.

It doesn't have to work out the first try.

Keep a positive mindset and keep trying.

Leave your past in the past.

Don't ever dwell on your past.

It made you who you are today.

Now is the time to focus on the present.

Build a better future.

Always wear a smile.

Life is too short.

Wear a smile and wear it proudly.

Never care what others think.

You do you.

Focus on your goals.

Live your life to its fullest.

What others think does not matter.

Live your life every day, as if it is your last.

You

I feel your touch.

Your hand on mine.

I need your touch.

Your lips, on mine.

Your touch.

Your body.

Your lips.

I yearn for more.

Your body against mine.

Your heart.

Your soul.

Your love.

I want all of you, always.

Your love.

My love.

Your soul.

My soul.

Your touch.

My touch.

You.

Hurt

Why did you hurt me?
Why did you yell?
Why are you mad?

Did I do something?
I must have.
I hurt you.

Maybe not physically.
Maybe it was more.
Emotionally and mentally.

If I say, I'm sorry.
If I change my ways.
If I listen better.

Will that make a difference?
Will you forgive me?

I don't like seeing you mad.
I don't like seeing you upset.

I hurt you.

I did not listen.

You got mad and hurt me back,

We can move on.

We can grow from this.

Try harder.

Hurt.

It affects everybody.

One Love

One body.

One soul.

We are a perfect match.

You were made for me.

I was made for you.

There is no other I will ever love.

There is no other who will know my soul as

you do.

We have become:

One body.

One soul.

One love.

The Man

Is he real?

Is he kind?

Is he heartfelt?

Is he pure?

Do not settle for anything less.

Is he honest?

Is he truthful?

Is he meaningful?

He should be all these things and more.

The right man, the perfect man.

A man should not hurt you.

He should not put you down.

He should be your other half, your better half.

Working together.

There to help you.

Your perfect and forever teammate.